THE LITTLE BOOK OF

Teatime Recipes

THE LITTLE BOOK OF
Teatime
Recipes

lesley mackley

AURA

© Salamander Books, 2007
10 Southcombe Street, London W14 0RA
An imprint of Anova Books Company Ltd

Printed and bound in China

All correspondence concerning the content of this volume should
be addressed to Salamander Books.

ILLUSTRATIONS: FINOLA STACK

ISBN 13: 978 1 905765 16 4

Contents

Introduction

Afternoon tea is the perfect way of entertaining either a few friends, or a large crowd, and can be anything from an intimate gathering around a roaring fire on a winter's afternoon, to a relaxed party in the garden on a sunny summer's day. In an age where everyone seems short of time, what could be more enjoyable than taking time to indulge in what was once part of everyday life, but has now become a luxury—afternoon tea.

The Little Book of Teatime Recipes has treats for every occasion. Some are old-fashioned favourites, guaranteed to bring back nostalgic memories, and alongside are recipes our Victorian and Edwardian ancestors would certainly not recognize, but which are welcome additions to any tea table.

So, bring out your prettiest tablecloth and best china, and indulge your family and friends with a delightful treat.

The History of Afternoon Tea

The custom of afternoon tea is thought to have been introduced in England in 1840 by Anna, the seventh Duchess of Bedford. Lunch was taken earlier then, and dinner was not served until about 9 O'clock. Not surprisingly, the Duchess became rather hungry during the afternoon and requested some tea, bread and butter and cake to be brought to her room. This quickly became a habit, and she started asking friends to join her.

It was soon fashionable to "take tea" in the middle of the afternoon, and the occasion became increasingly elaborate. Elegant tea accessories became available in the form of bone china tea services and delicate lace tablecloths, and the ladies would change into long tea gowns to preside over ornate silver teapots while engaging in lightweight conversation.

In Edwardian times, tea shops flourished and tea rooms in department stores became popular. Fashionable hotels serving elegant afternoon teas were popular meeting places.

Afternoon tea began to lose favour after World War II. Life is lived at a faster pace today, often making it impractical to stop in the middle of the afternoon for a leisurely cup of tea and cake. However, it is a habit well worth reviving, if only at the weekends, for an occasional moment of pure self-indulgence.

Making Afternoon Tea

Afternoon tea should be a graceful event; an opportunity to display the best china and table linen, and a time for people of all ages to gather together for relaxation and refreshments.

The choice of food served for afternoon tea depends on the occasion, the time of year and personal taste. A traditional tea consists of a selection of sandwiches and savouries, followed by scones or cookies and preserves, pastries, cookies, a simple cake, with a more elaborate cake as a centre-piece. At a winter's fireside, tea, toast and crumpets or muffins would be served with butter and savoury or sweet spreads.

The essential drink is, of course, tea, but many other drinks are also traditionally served, depending on the time of year. In the summer, iced tea, fruit cordials and cups are very refreshing, and in the winter, spiced tea or warming punches are always popular.

Making Tea

The type of tea you serve is a matter of personal taste, but it is a good idea to offer a choice of Indian or China tea, or a fragrant Earl Grey or Lapsong Souchong. Herbal or fruit teas are also becoming increasingly popular. China and other delicately flavoured teas should be served with slices of lemon, rather than milk.

It is certainly worth taking the trouble to produce a good cup of tea.

Making Tea

- Use the best quality tea you can afford.
- Fill the kettle with cold water.
- Warm the pot by rinsing with hot water.
- Use 1 teaspoon of tea for every 3 or 4 cups water.
- When the water is boiling, pour it onto the tea, replace the lid and steep to 5 minutes.
- Only serve tea that is freshly made.

Cucumber & Dill Hearts

1/4 cucumber
1/2 teaspoon wine vinegar
1/2 teaspoon salt
1 1/2 ounces butter, softened

4 slices white bread
Pepper
1 teaspoon chopped fresh dill
TO GARNISH: Dill sprigs

1 With a knife, peel cucumber, then cut into paper-thin slices. Place in a colander and sprinkle with vinegar and salt. Leave 30 minutes.

2 Pat cucumber slices dry on paper towels. Butter bread. Arrange cucumber slices on buttered sides of 2 bread slices. Season with pepper and scatter chopped dill over cucumber. Cover with remaining bread slices, buttered sides down, and press together.

3 Using a heart-shaped biscuit cutter, cut out 4 heart shapes from each sandwich. Arrange on a serving plate and garnish with dill sprigs.

Makes 8.

Egg & Cress Circles

4 eggs
4 tablespoons mayonnaise
1 teaspoon Dijon mustard
2 teaspoons Worcestershire
    sauce

Few drops hot-pepper sauce
Salt and pepper
3 ounces butter, softened
8 large slices white bread
Cress

1 To a saucepan, add eggs and enough water to cover eggs. Bring to a boil, reduce heat and simmer 12 minutes.

2 Drain eggs, crack shells lightly and place into a bowl of cold water until completely cold. Remove shells and coarsely chop eggs. Add mayonnaise, mustard, Worcestershire sauce, hot-pepper sauce, salt and pepper. Mix together well.

3 Butter bread. Spread egg mixture on buttered sides of 4 bread slices. Top with cress. Cover with remaining bread slices, buttered sides down, and press together. With a knife, cut off crusts from bread. Using a 2-inch round cookie cutter, cut out 4 circles from each sandwich. Arrange on a serving plate and garnish with cress.

Makes 16.

Striped Sandwiches

3 ounces sliced cooked ham
4 teaspoons mayonnaise
1/2 teaspoon Dijon mustard
2 ounces cream cheese
4 teaspoons chopped fresh
   chives

Salt and pepper
5 ounces butter, softened
2 slices white bread
2 slices wholemeal bread
TO GARNISH: Fresh chives

1 With a knife, finely chop ham. Into a bowl, place ham, mayonnaise and mustard. Mix together well.

2 In another bowl, mix together cream cheese, chives, salt and pepper. Butter 2 slices of white and wholemeal bread on one side only and the remaining 2 slices of white and wholemeal bread on both sides.

3 Spread half the ham mixture on buttered sides of 2 wholemeal bread slices. Cover with white bread which has been buttered on both sides. Spread cream cheese mixture over white bread. Cover with brown bread which has been buttered on both sides, spread with remaining ham mixture and top with white bread, buttered side down. Remove crusts from bread. Cut each sandwich into 6 pieces. Arrange on a serving plate and garnish with chives.

Makes 12.

Avocado & Bacon Sandwiches

4 ounces bacon slices
1 ripe avocado
1/2 teaspoon lemon juice
Salt and pepper
2 ounces butter, softened

4 large slices wholemeal
    bread
TO GARNISH: Lemon twist and
    parsley sprig

1 With a knife, coarsely chop bacon. Put into a skillet over medium heat and fry until bacon is crisp. Drain on paper towels.

2 Peel avocado, taking care not to remove bright green flesh just inside skin. Cut in half and remove seed. In a bowl; mash avocado, then stir in lemon juice, salt and pepper.

3 Butter bread. Spread avocado mixture on buttered sides of 2 bread slices. Scatter bacon over avocado. Cover with remaining bread slices, buttered sides down, and press together. With a knife, cut off crusts, cut each sandwich into 4 triangles. Arrange on a serving plate, garnished with a lemon twist and parsley sprig or cherry tomatoes.

Makes 8.

13

Turkey Triangles

2 ounces butter, softened
4 slices white bread
4 crisp lettuce leaves
3 ounces boneless cooked
    turkey, thinly sliced

Salt and pepper
4 teaspoons cranberry sauce
TO GARNISH: Small pickles,
    cut into fan shapes

1 Butter the bread. Arrange the lettuce leaves over buttered sides of 2 bread slices.

2 Arrange sliced turkey over lettuce. Season with salt and pepper to taste. Spread cranberry sauce over remaining bread slices, then place cranberry side down over turkey. Press together.

3 With a sharp knife, cut off crusts from bread. Cut each sandwich into 4 triangles. Arrange on a serving plate, garnish with pickles.

Makes 8.

Variation: Cranberry jelly may be used instead of cranberry sauce, if desired.

Salmon Pinwheels

1 large, unsliced sandwich loaf	Pepper
2 ounces butter, softened	1 teaspoon lemon juice
2 ounces watercress	To Garnish: Watercress
4 ounces thinly-sliced smoked salmon	

1 With a sharp knife, cut crusts from loaf of bread. Cut 2 (2-inch-thick) lengthwise slices from loaf. Using a rolling pin, roll each slice of bread firmly to flatten.

2 Spread butter over slices of bread. Remove stems from watercress and arrange leaves over buttered sides of slices. Arrange slices of smoked salmon over watercress. Season with pepper and sprinkle with lemon juice.

3 Roll up each slice, like a Swiss roll, starting from a short side. Wrap rolls tightly in plastic wrap and refrigerate for at least 2 hours. Remove plastic wrap and cut each roll into 7 pinwheels. Arrange on a serving plate, garnished with watercress.

Makes 14.

Stilton & Pear Pockets

4 pitta breads
2 ripe pears
2 ounces Stilton cheese,
    crumbled

6 ounces chopped walnuts
To Garnish: Lettuce leaves

1 Preheat grill. Grill or toast pitta breads lightly so they puff up. Cut each pitta bread in half, through the centre. Open each half to make a pocket.

2 Peel pears, remove cores and chop flesh coarsely. In a bowl, combine pears with crumbled Stilton cheese and chopped walnuts and mix together.

3 Divide pear mixture among pitta pockets. Arrange on a serving plate, garnished with lettuce leaves. Serve at once.

Makes 8.

Devilled ham Toasts

4 ounces lean cooked ham
1 tablespoon Worcestershire
    sauce
Red (cayenne) pepper, to taste
2 tablespoons Dijon mustard

6 slices bread
2 ounces butter, softened
TO GARNISH: 3 pimento-
    stuffed olives, sliced
Watercress sprigs

1 With a sharp knife, chop ham very finely, or mince. In a bowl, mix together ham, Worcestershire sauce, cayenne and mustard.

2 Toast bread. Using a 2-inch plain, round biscuit cutter, cut out 2 circles from each slice of toast. Butter each circle of toast using 2 tablespoons of the butter and keep warm. In a saucepan, melt remaining butter. Add ham mixture. Cook, stirring over a low heat until mixture is hot.

3 Spread ham mixture over toast circles. Garnish with olives and arrange on a serving plate with watercress garnish. Serve at once.

Makes 12 servings.

Crab & Ginger Triangles

1 (7-ounce) tin crabmeat,
   drained
6 green onions, finely chopped
1-inch piece ginger root,
   peeled and grated
2 teaspoons soy sauce

Salt and pepper
6 large sheets filo pastry, each
   about 14 inches square
3 ounces butter, melted
To Garnish: Spring onions.

1 In a bowl, mix together crabmeat, green onions, ginger root, soy sauce, salt and pepper. Set aside.

2 Preheat oven to 350F (175C). Lightly grease a baking sheet. Work with 1 sheet of pastry at a time, keeping remainder covered with a damp cloth. Cut sheet of pastry in half. Brush each half with melted butter and fold in half lengthwise. Brush pastry all over with melted butter. Put a portion of crab mixture in 1 corner of 1 strip of pastry. Fold pastry and filling over at right angles to make a triangle, and then continue folding in this way along strip of pastry to make a triangular package.

3 Repeat with remaining pastry and crab mixture. Brush each triangle with melted butter. Bake for 20 to 25 minutes, until crisp and golden brown. Serve warm, garnished with spring onion.

Makes 12.

Tuna Toasties

1 (7-ounce) tin tuna
3 tomatoes
3 ounces Cheddar cheese

4 slices bread
1 ounce butter, softened
TO GARNISH: Dill sprigs

1 Preheat oven to 400F (250C). Drain tuna. Place tuna in a bowl and flake. With a knife, slice tomatoes. Grate cheese.

2 Spread one side of each slice of bread with butter. Place buttered sides down on a baking sheet.

3 Spread tuna over bread. Arrange tomatoes on top and cover with shredded cheese. Bake 8 to 10 minutes, until bubbling. Cool for 1 minute, then cut each slice of bread across into 2 triangles. Serve hot, garnished with dill.

Makes 8.

Parmesan Beignets

2 ounces butter
3 ounces plain flour, sifted
2 eggs, beaten
1 teaspoon chopped fresh
  parsley
2 ounces grated Parmesan
  cheese

1 ounce grated Cheddar
  cheese
Salt and pepper
Vegetable oil for deep frying
TO GARNISH: Parsley sprigs

1 In a large pan, melt butter. Add 5 fluid ounces of water and bring to the
boil.

2 Add flour all at once and beat thoroughly until mixture leaves the side of the pan.
Cool slightly, then vigorously beat in eggs, a little at a time. Stir in parsley, cheeses,
salt and pepper. Continue beating until cheeses have melted.

3 One-third fill a deep-fat fryer with vegetable oil and heat to 360F (180C). Carefully
drop 4 or 5 walnut-size spoonfuls of dough into hot oil. Deep-fry for 2 to 3
minutes, until puffed and golden brown. Drain well on paper towels and keep warm
until all the beignets are fried. Serve garnished with parsley sprigs.

Makes about 16.

Welsh Rarebit/Rabbit Fingers

8 ounces mature Cheddar
  cheese
1 ounce butter, softened
1 tablespoon Worcestershire
  sauce
1 teaspoon mustard powder
1 tablespoon plain flour

About 2 fluid ounces beer
4 slices wholemeal bread
TO GARNISH: Red (cayenne)
  pepper for dusting
Red pepper strips
Parsley sprigs

1 Preheat grill. Grate the cheese into a bowl. Add butter, Worcestershire sauce, mustard, flour and enough beer to make a stiff paste.

2 Toast bread on both sides. Spread cheese mixture over one side of each slice of toast.

3 Grill until topping is cooked through and well browned. Dust with cayenne pepper. Cut each slice of toast into 3 rectangles. Garnish with pepper strips and parsley sprigs.

Makes 12.

Mini Quiches

1½ packets shortcrust pastry
3 egg yolks
1 egg
Salt and pepper to taste
10 fluid ounces whipping
cream

MUSHROOM FILLING:
½ ounce butter
4 ounces finely-chopped
mushrooms
PEPPER FILLING:
½ ounce butter
1 red pepper, chopped

1 Preheat oven to 400F (205C). Grease 12 individual 2½-inch quiche moulds.

2 To make mushroom filling; in a small pan, melt the 1 tablespoon butter. Add mushrooms and cook gently until softened and all liquid has evaporated. Set aside. To make pepper filling; in another small pan, melt remaining 1 tablespoon butter. Add pepper and cook gently until beginning to soften. Set aside. On a floured surface, roll out pastry to ⅛-inch thick. Use to line prepared pans; prick bottoms with fork.

3 Press a square of foil into each dough case. Bake blind for 15 minutes, removing foil after 12 minutes. In a bowl, beat together egg yolks, egg, salt, pepper and cream. Put half the mixture in a bowl with the mushrooms and half in a bowl with the red pepper. Divide the 2 fillings among baked pastry shells. Return to oven and cook for 15 minutes longer, just until firm. Serve warm or at room temperature.

Makes 12.

Cheese Straws

4 ounces plain flour
Pinch of salt
1/2 teaspoon curry powder
2 ounces butter, chilled

2 ounces grated Cheddar
   cheese
1 egg, beaten
TO FINISH: Poppy seeds and
   cumin seeds

1 Into a bowl, sift flour, salt and curry powder. Cut in butter until mixture resembles fine bread crumbs. Add cheese and half of the egg and mix to form a dough. Cover and refrigerate for at least 30 minutes.

2 Preheat oven to 400F (205C). Butter several baking sheets. On a floured surface, roll out dough to 1/4-inch thick. Cut into 3" x 1/2" strips. Twist and place on baking sheets.

3 Brush cheese straws with remaining egg. Sprinkle half with poppy seeds and half with cumin seeds. Bake 10 to 15 minutes, until golden.

Makes 24 to 30.

Scotch Eggs

1/2 pound pork sausage meat	Plain flour for coating
1 tablespoon chopped fresh chives	1 egg, beaten
Salt and pepper	6 ounces fresh white bread crumbs
8 hard-boiled quails' eggs	Vegetable oil for deep-frying

1 Into a bowl, put sausage. Mix in chives, salt and pepper. Divide into 8 equal portions. On a floured surface, flatten each piece into a 2-inch circle.

2 Shell eggs and dust with flour. Put beaten egg in one dish and bread crumbs in another. Place each egg on a circle of sausage. Mould sausage around egg, sealing seams well.

3 Roll each sausage-covered egg in beaten egg, then bread crumbs. One-third fill a deep-fat fryer with vegetable oil and heat to 306F (180C). Carefully put eggs into oil and deep-fry for 3 to 4 minutes, until golden brown. Drain well on paper towels until cool.

Makes 8.

Variation: Instead of quails' eggs, use 4 chicken eggs and cook 5 to 6 minutes.

Scones

8 ounces self-raising flour, plus extra for dusting	5 teaspoons sugar
1 teaspoon baking powder	5 fluid ounces milk
2 ounces butter, chilled	To Serve: Butter or whipped cream and jam

1 Preheat oven to 425F (220C). Dust a baking sheet with flour. Into a bowl, sift flour and baking powder, then stir to mix. Cut in butter, then stir in sugar.

2 Make a well in the centre of the mixture and pour in milk. Using a knife, mix together until dough is soft, but not sticky. Turn out dough onto a floured surface and knead lightly. Pat dough out to $1/2$-inch thick.

3 Using a 2-inch round biscuit cutter, cut out 12 scones. Arrange on prepared baking sheet and dust the tops with flour. Bake for 10 to 12 minutes, until well risen and light brown. Transfer to a wire rack and cover with a cloth while cooling. Serve with butter or whipped cream and jam.

Makes 12.

Variation: For cheese scones, omit sugar and stir in 2 ounces grated Cheddar cheese.

Scotch Pancakes

8 ounces self-raising flour
2 teaspoons baking powder
Pinch of salt
5 teaspoons sugar
1 egg, beaten
½ pint milk

ORANGE BUTTER:
6 ounces unsalted butter,
    softened
2 tablespoons icing sugar,
2 tablespoons fresh orange
    juice
Shredded zest of ½ orange

1 To make orange butter; in a bowl, beat together all ingredients until light and fluffy. To make pancakes, into another bowl, sift flour, baking powder and salt. Stir in sugar and make a well in centre. In another bowl, mix together egg and milk, then pour into the well. Gradually draw flour into liquid by stirring with a wooden spoon, then beat to make a smooth batter.

2 Slowly heat a greased griddle or heavy-bottomed skillet. Drop spoonfuls of batter onto hot pan and cook for about 3 minutes, until bubbles burst on surface and underside is golden. Turn pancakes over with a spatula and cook 1 minute longer, until golden on second side. Wrap in a cloth to keep warm until all pancakes are cooked. Serve with orange butter.

Makes 20 to 24.

Apple Biscuit Round

8 ounces plain flour
2 teaspoons baking powder
4 ounces butter, chilled
2 dessert apples
4 ounces caster sugar

3 ounces sultanas
1 egg, beaten
TO FINISH: 1 tablespoon
   demerara sugar
TO SERVE: Butter

1 Preheat oven to 350F (175C). Grease an 8-inch round cake tin. Into a bowl, sift flour and baking powder.

2 Put in butter until mixture resembles bread crumbs. Peel and core apples, cut into small dice and stir into flour and butter mixture with sugar and golden raisins. Stir in beaten egg to form a soft dough. Press mixture into prepared pan. Sprinkle brown sugar on top.

3 Bake for 40 to 50 minutes, until well risen and golden brown. Turn out onto wire rack and leave until just warm. Cut biscuit in half horizontally. Spread bottom with butter and replace top. Cut into wedges and serve.

Makes 8 wedges.

Blackberry Muffins

10 ounces plain flour
1 tablespoon baking powder
4 ounces caster sugar
1 egg
10 fluid ounces milk

3 fluid ounces vegetable oil
1 teaspoon vanilla extract
6 ounces blackberries
TO FINISH: 2 tablespoons
     demerara sugar

1 Preheat oven to 400F (205C). Grease a 12-cup muffin pan. Into a bowl, sift flour and baking powder. Stir in sugar.

2 In another bowl, beat together egg, milk, oil and vanilla. Add to dry ingredients all at once. Stir just until blended. Gently stir in blackberries.

3 Spoon batter into prepared muffin pan. Sprinkle with brown sugar. Bake 15 to 20 minutes, until well risen and golden-brown. Cool in pan 5 minutes, then turn out muffins on to a wire rack to cool completely.

Makes 12.

Chocolate Nut Muffins

4 ounces plain chocolate
8 ounces plain flour
1 tablespoon baking powder
1/2 teaspoon ground cinnamon
3 ounces soft brown sugar

4 ounces coarsely-chopped
   walnuts
1/2 pint milk
2 fluid ounces vegetable oil
1 teaspoon vanilla extract
1 egg

1 Preheat oven to 400F (205C). Grease a 12-cup cake tin.

2 Into a heatproof bowl—set over a pan of simmering water—break the chocolate and heat until melted. Remove from heat.

3 Into bowl of chocolate, sift flour, baking powder and cinnamon. Add sugar and nuts. In another bowl, mix together milk, oil, vanilla and egg. Add to dry ingredients and stir just until blended. Spoon batter into prepared pan. Bake for 15 to 20 minutes, until well risen and firm to touch. Cool in pan for 5 minutes, then turn out muffins onto a wire rack to cool completely.

Makes 12.

Welsh Cakes

8 ounces self-raising flour
Pinch of salt
2 ounces white cooking fat
2 ounces margarine, chilled
3 ounces caster sugar

3 ounces dried currants
1 egg, beaten
1 tablespoon milk (optional)
TO FINISH: Sugar for dusting

1 Into a bowl, sift flour and salt. Cut in cooking fat and margarine until mixture resembles bread crumbs. Stir in sugar and currants.

2 Add egg and a little milk, if necessary, to make a soft, but not sticky dough. On a floured surface, roll out dough to 1/4-inch thick. Using 2 1/2-inch plain or fluted round biscuit cutter, cut out about 16 circles.

3 Heat a greased griddle or heavy-bottomed skillet. Cook cakes over low heat, about 3 minutes on each side until golden brown.
Dust with Sugar

Makes about 16.

Date & Walnut Loaf

8 ounces stoned dates
Grated zest and juice of
    1 lemon
3 fluid ounces water
6 ounces butter, softened

6 ounces soft brown
    sugar
3 eggs, beaten
6 ounces self-raising flour
2 ounces chopped walnuts
TO FINISH: 8 walnut halves

1 Preheat oven to 325F (170C). Grease and line the bottom of 9" x 5" loaf tin with waxed paper. Chop dates.

2 Into a saucepan, put dates with lemon zest and juice and water. Cook for 5 minutes, until a soft puree. In a bowl, beat butter and sugar together until light and fluffy. Gradually beat in eggs. Fold in flour and chopped walnuts. Spread one-third of batter over bottom of prepared pan. Spread half the date puree over batter. Repeat layers, ending with cake batter.

3 Arrange halved walnuts in a line down centre of loaf. Bake for 1 to 1½ hours, until well risen and firm to the touch. Cool loaf in tin for 10 minutes, then turn out loaf, peel off lining paper and transfer to a wire rack to cool completely. Serve sliced.

Makes 10 to 12 slices.

Cheese & Chive Braid

1 pound bread flour
1 teaspoon salt
1 teaspoon sugar
1½ teaspoons active dry yeast
2 ounces butter, chilled
4 ounces grated Cheddar
    cheese

3 tablespoons chopped
    fresh chives
4 spring onions, chopped
5 fluid ounces lukewarm milk
6 fluid ounces lukewarm water
TO GLAZE: Beaten egg

1 Into a bowl, sift flour. Stir in salt, sugar and yeast. Cut in butter.

2 Stir cheese, chives and spring onions and make a well in the centre. Mix milk with water, then pour into the well. Mix until a soft dough is formed. Turn out dough onto a lightly-floured surface. Knead about 10 minutes, until smooth and elastic. Place in an oiled bowl, cover and leave in a warm place about 1 hour, until doubled in bulk. Turn dough out onto a floured surface and knead about 3 minutes.

3 Divide dough into 3 pieces. Roll each one out to a long rope and braid together, pinching ends to seal. Place on a baking sheet, cover with oiled plastic wrap and leave in a warm place for about 45 minutes, until doubled in bulk. Preheat oven to 425F (220C). Brush with beaten egg and bake 20 minutes. Reduce temperature to 350F (175C) and bake 15 minutes longer, until golden brown and the bottom sounds hollow when tapped. Serve warm or cold with cheese and salad.

Makes about 10 slices.

Chelsea Buns

8 ounces bread flour
2 teaspoons active dry yeast
1 teaspoon sugar
1/2 teaspoon salt
2 ounces unsalted butter, chilled
1/4 pint lukewarm milk
1 egg, beaten

FILLING: 2 ounces unsalted butter, softened
4 ounces brown sugar
5 ounces chopped mixed dry fruit
1 teaspoon apple pie spice
TO FINISH: 4 ounces icing sugar

1 Butter an 8-inch square cake tin. Into a bowl, sift flour. Stir in yeast, sugar and salt. Cut in butter. Make a well in centre. Pour in milk and egg and beat vigorously to make a soft dough. On a floured surface, knead dough 5 to 10 minutes, until smooth. Put dough in an oiled bowl, cover and leave in a warm place for about 1 hour, until doubled in bulk. Turn dough out onto a floured surface. Knead lightly. Roll out to a 12" x 9" rectangle.

2 Spread with butter, then sprinkle with brown sugar, fruit and spice. Roll up from a long side and cut into 9 pieces. Place in pan, cut sides uppermost. Cover with oiled plastic wrap. Leave in a warm place 45 minutes, until almost doubled in bulk. Preheat oven to 375F (190C). Bake 30 minutes, until golden. Cool in pan 10 minutes, then turn out and transfer in one piece to a wire rack to cool. Mix icing sugar with enough water to make a thin glaze. Brush over buns. Leave to cool.

Makes 9.

Lemon & Currant Brioches

8 ounces bread flour
2 teaspoons active dry yeast
1/2 teaspoon salt
1 tablespoon sugar
2 ounces dried currants
Grated zest of 1 lemon

2 tablespoons lukewarm water
2 eggs, beaten
2 ounces unsalted butter,
    melted
TO GLAZE: 1 egg, beaten

1 Butter 12 individual brioche moulds. Into a bowl, sift flour. Stir in yeast, salt, sugar, currants and lemon zest.

2 Make a well in centre. Pour in water, eggs and melted butter and beat vigorously to make a soft dough. Turn dough out onto a lightly-floured surface and knead 5 minutes, until smooth and elastic. Put dough in an oiled bowl, cover and leave in a warm place 1 hour, until doubled in bulk. Turn dough out onto a lightly-floured surface, knead again and roll into a rope shape. Cut into 12 equal pieces. Shape three quarters of each piece into a ball and place in prepared moulds.

3 With a floured finger, press a hole in centre of each. Shape remaining dough into little plugs, then press into holes, flattening the tops slightly. Place moulds on a baking sheet. Cover with oiled plastic wrap and leave in warm place until dough comes almost to top of moulds. Preheat oven to 425F (220C). Brush brioches with beaten egg. Bake for 15 minutes, until golden brown. Serve warm.

Makes 12.

Crumpets

1 pound bread flour
1 teaspoon salt
1 teaspoon sugar
2 teaspoons active dry yeast

20 fluid ounces lukewarm milk
5 fluid ounces lukewarm water
Vegetable oil for cooking
TO SERVE: Butter and jam

1 Into a bowl, sift flour. Stir in salt, sugar and yeast.

2 Make a well in the centre of the flour and pour in milk and water. With a wooden spoon, gradually work flour into liquid, then beat vigorously to make smooth batter. Cover bowl with a cloth and leave in a warm place 1 hour or until batter has doubled in bulk.

3 Thoroughly grease a heavy skillet or griddle and several crumpet rings or round biscuit cutters. Arrange as many rings as possible in pan. Heat pan, then pour in enough batter to half fill each ring. Cook crumpets for 5 to 6 minutes, until bubbles appear and burst on the surface. Remove rings and turn crumpets over. Cook on other side 2 to 3 minutes longer. Return rings to skillet to heat and repeat with remaining batter. Serve crumpets hot, generously buttered, with jam.

Makes about 16.

Devonshire Splits

2 ounces unsalted butter
2 tablespoons sugar
5 fluid ounces milk
5 fluid ounces water
1 pound bread flour
2 teaspoons active dry yeast
½ teaspoon salt

FILLING: 4 ounces strawberry
   jam
10 fluid ounces whipping
   cream
TO FINISH: Icing sugar
   for dusting

1 In a saucepan, heat butter, sugar, milk and water, until the sugar has dissolved.

2 Let mixture stand until lukewarm (130F, 55C). Into a bowl, stir flour. Stir in yeast and salt. Make a well in the centre, then pour in liquid and mix vigorously to make a soft dough. On a lightly-floured surface, turn out dough and knead until smooth. Place in an oiled bowl; cover and leave in a warm place until doubled in bulk. Grease 2 baking sheets.

3 Turn dough out onto a floured surface. Divide into 16 pieces. Knead each piece lightly and shape into ball. Place on baking sheets, flattening each ball slightly. Cover with oiled plastic wrap and leave in warm place for about 40 minutes, until well risen. Preheat oven to 425F (220C). Bake about 15 minutes, until bottoms sound hollow when tapped. Cool on wire rack. Split and fill with jam and cream. Dust lightly with icing sugar.

Makes 16.

Lemon Crunch Cake

4 ounces butter or margarine,
  softened
6 ounces caster sugar
2 eggs, beaten
Finely grated zest of 1 lemon

6 ounces self-raising flour,
  sifted
4 fluid ounces milk
TOPPING: Juice of 1 lemon
4 ounces sugar

1 Preheat oven to 350F (175C). Grease a 9" x 7" or an 8-inch square baking tin and line with waxed paper. In a bowl, beat together butter and sugar until light and fluffy.

2 Gradually beat in eggs. Stir in lemon zest. Fold in sifted flour alternately with milk. Pour batter into prepared pan and level surface with a metal spatula. Bake about 50 minutes, until well risen and pale golden.

3 While cake is baking, make topping. In a bowl, mix together lemon juice and sugar. Spoon topping over hot cake. Leave cake in pan until completely cold, then turn out cake and cut into squares or diamonds.

Makes 12 squares or diamonds.

Ginger Cake

8 ounces self-raising flour
1 tablespoon ground ginger
1 teaspoon ground cinnamon
1/2 teaspoon baking soda
4 ounces butter or margarine,
    chilled
6 ounces, soft brown sugar

2 eggs
5 teaspoons golden syrup
5 teaspoons milk
Topping: 3 pieces stem ginger
6 ounces icing sugar
4 teaspoons stem ginger syrup

1 Preheat oven to 325F (165C). Grease an 11" x 7" baking tin and line with waxed paper. Into a bowl, sift flour, ginger, cinnamon and baking soda. Cut in butter, then stir in sugar. In another bowl, beat together eggs, syrup and milk. Pour into dry ingredients and beat until smooth and glossy. Pour batter into pan. Bake for 45 to 50 minutes, until well risen and firm to touch. Cool in pan for 30 minutes, then transfer to wire rack to cool completely.

2 Cut each piece of stem ginger into quarters and arrange on top of cake. In a bowl, mix together icing sugar, ginger syrup and enough water to make a smooth frosting. Put frosting into a waxed-paper piping bag and drizzle frosting over top of cake. Leave to set. Cut cake into squares.

Makes 12 pieces.

Dundee Cake

8 ounces butter, softened
12 ounces soft brown sugar
4 eggs, beaten
10 ounces plain flour,
  sifted
5 fluid ounces milk
2 ounces ground blanched
  almonds
4 ounces dried currants
4 ounces golden raisins
4 ounces dark raisins

2 ounces chopped mixed
  citrus peel
2 ounces glacé cherries,
  halved
Grated zests of 1 small orange
  and 1 small lemon
1/2 teaspoon baking soda,
  dissolved in 1 teaspoon
  milk
2 ounces whole blanched
  almonds

1 Preheat oven to 325F (165C). Grease and line an 8-inch springform cake tin with waxed paper. In a bowl, beat butter and sugar until light and fluffy. Gradually beat in eggs. Fold in flour alternately with milk. Carefully fold in ground almonds, currants, golden raisins, raisins, peel, cherries and orange and lemon zests. Add baking soda dissolved in milk. Stir to mix.

2 Pour batter into prepared tin. Smooth top with a metal spatula. Arrange blanched almonds in concentric circles over top of cake. Bake for 2 1/2 to 3 hours, until a skewer inserted into centre of the cake comes out clean. Cool in pan for 30 minutes, then turn out cake, peel off lining paper and transfer to a wire rack to cool completely.

Makes about 12 slices.

Apple Streusel Cake

6 ounces self-raising flour
1 teaspoon baking powder
4 ounces margarine, softened
4 ounces sugar
2 eggs, beaten
1 or 2 tablespoons milk

TOPPING: 4 ounces self-raising
    flour
1 teaspoon ground cinnamon
3 ounces butter
4 ounces caster sugar
1 pound Granny Smith apples
A little lemon juice
TO FINISH: Icing sugar

1 Preheat oven to 350F (175C). Grease a 9-inch springform cake tin. To make topping, into a bowl, sift flour and cinnamon. Cut in butter until mixture resembles coarse crumbs. Stir in granulated sugar; set aside. Peel, core and thinly slice apples. Toss in a little lemon juice.

2 In another bowl, sift flour and baking powder. Add margarine, sugar and eggs. Beat well until mixture is smooth, adding just enough milk to make a good consistency. Spoon into prepared tin. Cover with apple slices and sprinkle with streusel topping. Bake for 1 hour until firm to the touch and golden brown. Cool in pan before opening sides. Dust with icing sugar.

Makes 8 to 10 slices.

Note: Keep cake 24 hours before serving.

Honey Spice Cake

5 ounces butter or margarine	1½ teaspoons apple pie spice (mixed spice)
4 ounces soft brown sugar	2 eggs, beaten
6 ounces clear honey	FROSTING: 12 ounces icing sugar
1 tablespoon water	About 3 tablespoons water
7 ounces self-raising flour	

1 Preheat oven to 350F (175C). Grease a fluted ring mould with a 2 pint capacity. Into a saucepan, put butter, sugar, honey and water.

2 Heat gently until butter has melted and sugar has dissolved. Remove from heat and cool 10 minutes. Into a bowl, sift flour and apple pie spice. Pour in melted mixture and eggs; beat well until smooth. Pour batter into prepared pan. Bake for 40 to 50 minutes, until well risen and a skewer inserted into centre comes out clean. Cool cake in pan for 2 to 3 minutes, then turn out cake and transfer to a wire rack to cool completely.

3 To make frosting; into a bowl, sift icing sugar. Stir in enough water to make a smooth frosting. Carefully spoon frosting over cake so cake is evenly covered.

Makes 8 to 10 slices.

Toffee Date Cake

8 ounces chopped dates
10 fluid ounces boiling water
4 ounces butter, softened
6 ounces caster sugar
3 eggs, beaten
8 ounces self-raising flour, sifted

$^1/_2$ teaspoon ground cinnamon
1 teaspoon baking soda
1 teaspoon vanilla extract
TOPPING: 3 ounces soft brown sugar
2 ounces butter
3 tablespoons whipping cream

1 Preheat oven to 350F (175C). Grease a 9-inch springform tin. In a bowl, beat butter and sugar until light and fluffy. Gradually beat in eggs. Fold in flour and cinnamon. Add baking soda and vanilla to dates and water. Pour onto creamed mixture; stir until thoroughly mixed. Pour into prepared pan. Bake for 1 to 1$^1/_4$ hours, until well risen and firm to the touch. Meanwhile, preheat grill.

2 To make topping; into a saucepan, put brown sugar, butter and cream. Heat gently until sugar is melted. Bring to a boil, then simmer 3 minutes. Pour topping over cake and put under the grill until topping is bubbling. Cool in pan until toffee is set. Turn out cake, then transfer to a wire rack to cool completely.

Makes 8 to 10 slices.

Peach & Orange Cake

4 ounce tin of peach slices
6 ounces butter
8 ounces caster sugar
Grated zest of 1 orange
4 eggs, beaten

5 fluid ounces thick sour
  cream
8 ounces plain flour
$1/2$ teaspoon baking soda
TO FINISH: Icing sugar
Grated zest of 1 orange

1 Preheat oven to 175C. Grease a
kugelhopf mould and dust with flour.
Drain peach slices and coarsely chop.

2 In a bowl, beat butter and sugar until
light and fluffy. Add orange zest and
gradually beat in eggs. Fold in peaches
and sour cream. Sift flour and baking
soda onto batter. Fold in gently and
spread into prepared tin, smoothing the
top with a metal spatula. Bake for 45 to
50 minutes, until well risen and golden
brown.

3 Cool in pan for 10 minutes, then
turn out cake and transfer to a wire
rack to cool completely. Sift icing sugar
over cake. Decorate with orange zest.

Makes 8 to 10 slices.

Blackcurrant Whirls

8 ounces butter, softened
3 ounces icing sugar, sifted
Few drops almond extract
8 ounces plain flour

2 tablespoons blackcurrant
   jam
TO FINISH: Icing sugar for
   dusting

1 Preheat oven to 350F (175C). Arrange 12 paper cupcake cups in a muffin tin. In a bowl, beat butter with icing sugar and almond extract until creamy. Sift flour onto mixture and beat until smooth.

2 Spoon batter into a piping bag fitted with a large nozzle. Pipe whirls into paper cups, covering bottoms. Pipe a ring around edge to leave a slight hollow in centre.

3 Bake for 20 minutes until set and very lightly browned. Transfer from muffin tin to a wire rack to cool. Put a little jam in centre of each whirl. Dust lightly with icing sugar.

Makes 12.

Strawberry-Rose Meringues

2 egg whites
4 ounces sugar
FILLING:
10 fluid ounces whipping
cream

4 medium-size strawberries
2 teaspoons icing sugar
2 teaspoons rosewater
TO DECORATE: 12 strawberries

1 Preheat oven to 250F (120C). Line 2 baking sheets with parchment paper.

2 To make meringues; in a bowl, beat egg whites until soft peaks form. Slowly beat in sugar until stiff peaks form. Spoon meringue into a piping bag fitted with a large nozzle. Pipe 24 (3-inch) strips onto prepared baking sheets. Bake for 1 hour until dry and crisp. Cool on wire racks.

3 To make filling; in a bowl, whip cream until stiff peaks form. In a food processor or blender, process strawberries until smooth. Press through strainer into a bowl. Stir in icing sugar and rosewater. Add cream and mix well together. Sandwich meringues together with strawberry cream. Decorate with strawberries and serve at once.

Makes 12.

Honey Madeleines

2 ounces butter
2 eggs
2 ounces caster sugar
1 tablespoon honey

2 ounces plain flour
1/2 teaspoon baking powder
TO FINISH: Icing sugar for
sifting

1 Preheat oven to 375F (190C). Lightly butter 12 madeleine moulds (or jam tart tin). In a small saucepan over low heat, melt the butter. Cool.

2 In a bowl, beat eggs and sugar until pale and thick. Stir in melted butter and honey. Sift flour and baking powder onto egg mixture, then fold in.

3 Spoon mixture into prepared moulds. Bake for 10 minutes, until light golden brown. Leave in moulds for 2 minutes, then turn out and transfer to a wire rack to cool. Dust lightly with icing sugar.

Makes 12.

Chocolate Brownies

2 ounces plain flour
1 ounce cocoa powder
4 ounces butter
8 ounces caster sugar
1 teaspoon vanilla extract
2 eggs, beaten

2 ounces chopped walnuts
FROSTING: 4 ounces plain
    chocolate
5 fluid ounces sour cream

1 Preheat oven to 325F (165C). Butter an 8-inch square cake tin. Onto a plate, sift flour and cocoa powder.

2 Into a saucepan over low heat, put butter, sugar and 1 tablespoon cold water. Stir until butter melts. Remove from heat. Stir in vanilla, then beat eggs, one at a time. Add flour and cocoa powder and beat to a smooth, shiny batter. Stir in walnuts. Pour batter into prepared tin. Bake for 20 minutes, until set. Leave in tin to cool completely.

3 To make frosting; into a heatproof bowl—over a pan of simmering water—break chocolate. Heat until chocolate is melted. Stir until smooth then remove from heat. Stir in sour cream and beat until evenly blended. Spoon topping over brownies and make a swirling pattern with a spatula. Leave in a cool place to set. Cut into squares and remove from pan.

Makes 9 large or 16 small brownies.

Strawberry Shortcake

8 ounces plain flour
1 tablespoon baking powder
1 ounce caster sugar
3 ounces butter, chilled
3 fluid ounces milk

FILLING: 1½ pounds
strawberries
2 ounces caster sugar
10 fluid ounces whipping
cream

1 Preheat oven to 425F (220C). Grease a baking sheet. Into a bowl, sift flour and baking powder.

2 Stir in sugar. Cut in butter until mixture resembles bread crumbs. Pour in milk and mix to form a soft dough. Turn out dough onto a lightly-floured surface, then roll out to ¼-inch thick. Cut into 8 (3-inch) circles. Place on prepared baking sheet. Bake for 10 to 12 minutes, until golden brown. Slice most of strawberries, reserving a few for decorating. In a bowl, mix together sliced strawberries and sugar. In another bowl, whip cream until soft peaks form.

3 Split shortcakes in half while still warm. Spread bottom halves with two-thirds of the cream. Cover cream with sliced strawberries and top with other shortcake halves. Add a swirl of cream to each one and decorate with reserved strawberries.

Makes 8.

Ginger Brandy Snaps

2 ounces unsalted butter
2 ounces demerara sugar
2 tablespoons golden syrup
2 ounces pain flour
1/2 teaspoon ground ginger
1 teaspoon brandy

FILLING: 10 fluid ounces
 whipping cream
1 tablespoon stem ginger
 syrup
6 pieces stem ginger

1 Preheat oven to 350F (175C).

2 Grease several baking sheets. Butter the handles of 3 or 4 wooden spoons. Into a saucepan, over medium heat, put butter, brown sugar and syrup. Heat until butter melts. Cool slightly. Sift flour and ginger onto melted ingredients and stir in with brandy. Drop teaspoons of mixture, well spaced out, onto baking sheets. Bake for 7 to 10 minutes, until brandy snaps are golden.

3 Quickly remove brandy snaps from baking sheets and roll around spoon handles, leaving them in place until set. Slide off spoons and leave on wire racks until completely cool. In a bowl, beat cream with ginger syrup until stiff peaks form. Spoon cream into a piping bag fitted with a small star-shaped nozzle. Pipe into each end of brandy snaps. Slice stem ginger pieces and use to decorate brandy snaps. Refrigerate until ready to serve.

Makes about 18.

Sponge Drops

2 ounces plain flour
2 large eggs
2 ounces caster sugar
Caster sugar, for sprinkling

FILLING:
5 fluid ounces double cream
4 teaspoons red jam

1 Preheat oven to 375F (190C). Grease several baking sheets and line with grease-proof paper. Into a bowl, sift flour. In another bowl, beat together eggs and sugar until pale and thick.

2 Sift flour again onto egg mixture, then fold in very gently. Spoon batter into a piping bag fitted with a 1-inch plain tip. Pipe batter onto prepared baking sheets in 1½ inch circles. Sprinkle each circle with sugar. Bake 10 minutes, until golden. Slide paper with sponge drops still attached off baking sheet onto damp tea towel. Cool completely.

3 In a bowl, whip cream until stiff peaks form. Remove sponge drops from paper. Sandwich together in pairs with a little jam and whipped cream.

Makes 18.

Summer Sponge Cake

6 ounces butter, softened
6 ounces caster sugar
3 eggs, beaten
6 ounces self-raising flour
4 teaspoons boiling water
FILLING: 3 ounces unsalted
butter, softened

4 ounces icing sugar, sifted
Few drops vanilla essence
ICING: 6 ounces icing
sugar, sifted'
2 teaspoons lemon juice
TO DECORATE: Crystallised
flowers

1 Preheat oven to 350F (180C). Grease two 8-inch round cake tins and line bottoms with waxed paper. In a bowl, beat together butter and sugar until light and fluffy. Gradually beat in eggs, then fold in flour. Stir in the boiling water to make a soft batter. Divide batter between prepared pans. Bake 25 to 30 minutes, until cakes are lightly browned and spring back when pressed. Cool in pans 5 minutes, then turn out cakes, peel off lining paper and transfer to wire racks to cool.

2 To make filling; in a bowl, beat together butter and icing sugar. Stir in vanilla. Sandwich cakes together with filling. To make icing, in a bowl, mix together icing sugar, lemon juice and enough water to make a good consistency for spreading. Spread icing over cake top and decorate with crystallised flowers.

Makes 8 slices.

Strawberry Roulade

6 eggs
7 ounces caster sugar
2 teaspoons baking powder
6 ounces grounded almonds
FILLING: 5 ounces cream
  cheese

5 fluid ounces double cream
8 ounces strawberries
2 passion fruit
TO DECORATE: Icing sugar
A few whole strawberries

1 Preheat oven to 350F (180C). Grease a 15 x 10 inch Swiss roll tin and line with waxed paper.

2 Separate eggs. In a bowl, beat whites until stiff but not dry. In another bowl, beat together egg yolks and sugar until pale and thick. Mix baking powder thoroughly into ground almonds. Stir gently into yolk mixture, without over-mixing. Carefully fold in egg whites. Spread batter in tin. Bake 15 minutes, until firm. Cover with a towel and leave cake to cool in tin.

3 In a bowl, beat cream cheese and cream until soft peaks form. Reserve one-third. Mash half of the strawberries; chop remaining strawberries. Scoop out passion fruit flesh and stir into cream with mashed strawberries. Place a sheet of waxed paper on a flat surface; dust thickly with icing sugar. Turn roulade out onto paper. Peel off lining paper. Spread cream over roulade; sprinkle with chopped strawberries. Roll up and pipe reserved cream on top. Decorate with reserved strawberries.

Makes 6 to 8 servings.

Coffee-Caramel Cake

8 ounces self-raising flour
6 ounces butter, softened
6 ounces caster sugar
3 eggs, beaten
7 tablespoons strong coffee

ICING AND DECORATION:
4 fluid ounces milk
4 1/4 ounces butter
3 tablespoons caster sugar
1 1/4 pounds icing sugar
Chocolate-covered coffee
   beans

1 Preheat oven to 350F (175C). Grease two 8-inch round cake tins and line the
bottoms with waxed paper.

2 Into a bowl, sift flour 3 times and set aside. In another bowl, beat together butter and
sugar until light and fluffy. Gradually beat in eggs. Fold in flour alternately with
coffee. Divide batter between prepared pans and bake 30 minutes, until slightly shrinking
from sides of pans. Cool cakes in pans 5 minutes, then turn out cakes and transfer to
wire racks to cool completely. To make icing; in a saucepan, warm milk and butter.

3 In another heavy-bottomed saucepan, heat sugar over low heat until it dissolves and
turns a golden caramel. Off the heat, stir in a warm milk, taking care as it may
splatter. Return to the heat and stir until caramel has dissolved. Remove from heat.
Gradually stir in icing sugar, beating until icing is a smooth spreading consistency.
Sandwich cakes together with some icing over top and side. Decorate with coffee beans.

Makes 8 to 10 servings.

Double Chocolate Gâteau

8 ounces butter, softened
8 ounces caster sugar
4 eggs, beaten
6 ounces self-raising flour
2 ounces cocoa powder
FILLING: 9 fluid ounces
   whipping cream
5 ounces white chocolate

FROSTING: 12 ounces plain
   chocolate
5 ounces butter
3 fluid ounces double cream
TO DECORATE: 4 ounces
   plain chocolate
2 teaspoons each icing sugar
   and cocoa powder mixed

1 To make the filling, heat cream in a saucepan to just below boiling point. In a food processor, chop white chocolate. With motor running, pour hot cream through feed tube and process 10 to 15 seconds, until smooth. Transfer to a bowl, cover with plastic wrap and chill overnight. The next day after cake is ready to fill, beat filling until just beginning to hold soft peaks.

2 To make chocolate curls for decoration, in a heatproof bowl over a pan of simmering water, melt chocolate. Spread one-quarter of chocolate over a baking sheet. Refrigerate sheet a few minutes until chocolate loses its gloss and is just set, but not hard. Using a metal spatula, scrape off large curls of chocolate, transferring them to a baking sheet lined with waxed paper. Refrigerate until set. Make 3 more batches of curls in the same way.

3 Preheat oven to 350F (180C). Grease an 8-inch deep round cake tin and line bottom with waxed paper. In a bowl, beat together butter and sugar until light and fluffy. Gradually beat in eggs. Into another bowl, sift together flour and cocoa powder. Fold into mixture, then spoon into pan. Bake for 45 to 50 minutes, until cake springs

back when lightly pressed and a skewer inserted into centre come out clean. Cool in tin 5 minutes, then turn out cake, remove lining paper and transfer to a wire rack to cool completely.

4 To make frosting; in a heatproof bowl over a pan of simmering water, melt chocolate. Stir in butter and cream. Cool, stirring occasionally, until mixture is a thick spreading consistency.

5 With a serrated knife, slice cake horizontally into 3 layers. Sandwich layers together with white chocolate filling. Cover top and sides of cake with chocolate icing. Arrange chocolate curls over top of cake.

Makes 10 slices.

Pineapple Carrot Cake

6 ounces carrots, peeled and grated
3 ounces walnuts
15 ounce tin crushed pineapple
6 ounces light brown sugar
3 eggs
3 ounces plain flour
1 teaspoon bicarbonate soda

2 teaspoons baking powder
6 fluid ounces sunflower oil
ICING:
4 ounces cream cheese
2 ounces butter, softened
6 ounces icing sugar
Few drops vanilla essence
TO DECORATE: Crystallised pineapple

1 Preheat oven to 350F (180C). Grease a 9-inch cake tin and line bottom with waxed paper. Add carrots to a bowl. Chop walnuts; add to carrots. Drain pineapple and add to bowl with sugar and eggs. Sift flour, bicarbonate soda and baking powder into bowl. Add oil and beat thoroughly until blended. Pour into tin. Bake for 50 to 60 minutes, until well risen and a skewer inserted into centre comes out clean.

2 Cool cake in tin for 5 minutes, then turn out cake and transfer to a wire rack to cool completely. To make icing; in a bowl, beat together cream cheese, butter, icing sugar and vanilla until smooth. Spread over cake. Decorate with crystallised pineapple.

Makes 10 to 12 servings.

Chocolate-Orange Cake

2 small oranges
3 ounces plain chocolate
7 ounces self-raising flour
1¹/₂ teaspoons baking powder
6 ounces margarine, softened
6 ounces caster sugar

3 eggs, beaten
TO GLAZE: 8 ounces icing
  sugar
2 tablespoons orange juice
2 ounces plain chocolate

1 Preheat oven to 325F (160C). Thoroughly grease a 30 fluid ounces fluted or plain ring mould.

2 With a sharp knife, cut peel and pith from oranges. Cut oranges into sections by cutting down between membranes. Chop sections into small pieces, reserving as much juice as possible. Grate chocolate coarsely. Into a bowl, sift flour and baking powder. Add margarine, sugar, eggs and any reserved orange juice. Beat thoroughly until batter is smooth. Fold in chopped oranges and grated chocolate. Spoon batter into prepared mould.

3 Bake for 40 minutes, until well risen and golden-brown. Cool in mould for 5 minutes, then turn out cake and transfer to wire rack to cool completely. To make icing; into a bowl, sift icing sugar. Stir in enough orange juice to make a thin icing. Using a spoon, drizzle icing over cake. Into a heatproof bowl over pan of simmering water, break chocolate. Melt. Drizzle chocolate over cake. Let set.

Makes 8 to 10 slices.

Lemon Mousse Gâteau

3 eggs
4½ ounces caster sugar
Few drops vanilla essence
3 ounces plain flour
FILLING: Grated zest and juice
    of 2 lemons
2 teaspoons unflavoured
    gelatin powder

3 eggs, separated
4 ounces caster sugar
5 fluid ounces double cream
TO DECORATE: Icing sugar
Raspberries
Lemon geranium or raspberry
    leaves, if available.

1 Preheat oven to 350F (180C). Grease a 9-inch cake tin and line with waxed paper. To make cake; in a bowl, beat eggs and sugar together until very thick and light. Stir in vanilla, then soft flour onto mixture and fold in gently. Spoon into prepared tin and bake for 25 minutes, until golden and the cake springs back when lightly pressed. Turn cake out onto a wire rack covered with sugared waxed paper. Peel off lining paper and cool completely.

2 With a serrated knife, slice the cake horizontally into two layers. Wash and dry cake pan and line bottom and sides with waxed paper. Place 1 cake layer in bottom of tin.

3 To make mousse filling; into a bowl, put juice of 1 lemon and 1 tablespoon water. Sprinkle with gelatin. Let stand for 10 minutes to soften. In a bowl, beat together egg yolks, sugar and lemon zest until thick. Gradually beat in remaining lemon juice, keeping mixture as thick as possible.

4 Place bowl of gelatin over pan of simmering water until gelatin has dissolved. Immediately beat it into egg-yolk mixture. In a bowl, whip cream until it just holds its shape. Fold cream into egg mixture. Beat egg whites until stiff but not dry. Gently fold into mousse. Pour mixture into prepared pan. Level surface. Cover and refrigerate for 45 to 60 minutes, until lightly set. Place second layer of cake on top. Cover and refrigerate overnight.

5 To serve, remove sides of pan and carefully peel away paper. Place a flat plate on top of cake and quickly invert cake. Ease off bottom of pan. Dust cake with sifted icing sugar and decorate with raspberries and geranium or raspberry leaves, if using.

Make 8 to 10 servings.

Tia Maria Choux Ring

1 packet Choux Pastry
2 tablespoons plain flour
2 tablespoons cornflour
2 ounces caster sugar
10 fluid ounces milk
3 egg yolks

5 fluid ounces whipping
  cream
Coffee essence
2 teaspoons Tia Maria
4 ounces icing sugar, sifted

1 Preheat oven to 425F (220C). Spoon pastry into a pastry bag fitted with a half–inch plain tip.

2 Pipe a double 8-inch circle onto a paper-lined baking sheet. Bake choux ring 20 minutes. Reduce temperature to 350F (180C) and bake for 10 to 15 minutes longer, until golden-brown. Split horizontally, then cool on a wire rack. Into a bowl, sift flour and cornstarch. Stir in sugar and 2 tablespoons milk to make a thick paste. Beat in egg yolks. In a saucepan, heat remaining milk to just below boiling point. Pour onto egg mixture, stirring constantly.

3 Strain mixture back into saucepan, then cook over low heat, stirring constantly until thickened. Cover closely with plastic wrap and refrigerate until chilled. In a bowl, whip cream until stiff peaks form and fold into custard. Stir in 2 teaspoons of the coffee essence and Tia Maria. Sandwich choux rings together with coffee filling. In a bowl, mix together icing sugar, a few drops of coffee extract and about 1 tablespoon water. Spoon over cake and let set.

Makes 8 servings.

Almond Macaroons

2 egg whites
3 ounces ground almonds
4 ounces caster sugar

2 teaspoons cornflour
Few drops almond essence
12 blanched almond halves

1 Preheat oven to 350F (180C). Line 2 baking sheets with waxed paper. Reserve 2 teaspoons egg white. In a large bowl, put remaining egg whites and beat until soft peaks form.

2 Fold in ground almonds, sugar, cornflour and almond essence until mixture is smooth. Put 6 spoonfuls of mixture onto each baking sheet and flatten slightly. Place an almond half in centre of each macaroon. Brush lightly with reserved egg white.

3 Bake for 20 minutes, until very lightly browned. Cool on baking sheets. When cold, remove macaroons from paper.

Makes 12.

Summer Fruit Tartlets

7 ounces plain flour, sifted
2 ounces ground almonds
3 ounces icing sugar, sifted
4 ounces butter
1 egg yolk
1 tablespoon milk
FILLING: 8 ounces cream
    cheese

Caster sugar, to taste
12 ounces fresh summer
    fruits, such as red and
    blackcurrants, raspberries
    and wild strawberries
Redcurrant jelly or other red
    jelly, heated, to glaze

1 In a bowl, mix together flour, ground almonds and icing sugar. Cut in butter until mixture resembles bread crumbs. Add egg yolk and milk; work in with spatula. Then with fingers until dough binds together. Wrap pastry in plastic wrap and refrigerate for 30 minutes. Preheat oven to 400F (200C). On a floured surface, roll out pastry thinly. Line 12 deep tartlet tins or individual brioche moulds with dough; prick bottoms.

2 Press piece of foil into each pastry case, covering the edges. Bake for 10 to 15 minutes, until light golden-brown. Remove foil and bake for 2 to 3 minutes longer. Transfer to a wire rack to cool. To make filling; in a bowl, mix a spoonful of filling in each pastry shell. Arrange fruit on top, then brush with glaze and serve at once.

Makes 12.

Maple Pecan Tartlets

5 ounces plain flour
3 ounces butter
3 tablespoons icing sugar
1 egg yolk
1 teaspoon lemon juice
FILLING: 2 tablespoons
    maple syrup

5 fluid ounces double cream
4 ounces caster sugar
Pinch of cream of tartar
4 ounces chopped pecans
Pecan halves to decorate

1 To make pastry, into a bowl, sift flour. Cut in butter until mixture resembles bread crumbs.

2 Stir in icing sugar. Add egg yolk, lemon juice and about 1 teaspoon water to form a firm dough. Turn dough out onto a lightly floured surface. Knead lightly. Wrap in plastic wrap and refrigerate for 30 minutes. Preheat oven to 400F (200C). On a lightly floured surface, roll out pastry thinly. Line 14 tartlet tins with dough; prick bottoms. Press a piece of foil into each pastry shell. Bake for 10 to 15 minutes, until light golden-brown. Remove foil and bake for 2 to 3 minutes longer. Transfer to a wire rack to cool.

3 To make filling, mix half syrup with half the cream; set aside. In a pan, heat sugar, cream of tartar and 2½ fluid ounces of water until sugar dissolves. Bring to boil; boil until light golden. Stir in maple syrup and cream mixture. Cook until mixture reaches 240F (116C) on a thermometer, or forms a soft ball when dropped in cold water. Stir in remaining cream. Cool slightly. Brush syrup over edges of tartlets. Put pecans in tartlets. Spoon over toffee. Top with pecan halves.

Makes 14.

Nutty Filo Fingers

4 ounces ground hazelnuts	3 ounces unsalted butter
2 ounces granulated sugar	6 large sheets filo pastry
2 teaspoons orange-flower water	TO FINISH: Caster sugar, for dusting

1 Preheat oven to 350F (180C). Grease 2 baking sheets. In a bowl, mix together ground hazelnuts, sugar and orange-flower water.

2 In a saucepan, melt butter. Cut each sheet of pastry into 4 rectangles. Pile on top of each other and cover with a tea towel to prevent drying out. Working with 1 pile of pastry rectangles at a time, brush each piece with melted butter.

3 Spread 1 teaspoon of filling along a short end. Fold long sides in, folding slightly over filling. Roll up from filling end. Place on a prepared baking sheet with seam underneath. Brush with melted butter. Repeat with remaining pastry rectangles and filling. Bake for 20 minutes, or until very lightly coloured. Transfer to wire racks to cool; sprinkle with sugar.

Makes 24.

Spiced Apricot Squares

8 ounces plain flour
1 teaspoon mixed spice
4 ounces ground almonds
1 egg, beaten
8 ounces caster sugar

6 ounces butter, softened
4 ounces apricot jam
TO FINISH: Icing sugar, for
    sifting

1 Into a bowl, sift flour and spice. Add ground almonds, egg, sugar and butter. Mix well until thoroughly combined. Knead lightly. Wrap in plastic wrap and refrigerate for at least 30 minutes.

2 Butter a 11 x 7 inch baking tin. Into pan, press half of the dough. Spread apricot jam over dough. On a floured surface, lightly knead remaining dough. Roll out and cut into thin strips. Arrange strips over jam to form close lattice pattern. Refrigerate 30 minutes. Preheat oven to 350F (180C).

3 Bake for 30 to 40 minutes, until lightly browned. Cool cookies in pan, then sift icing sugar over top. Cut into 24 squares or bars.

Makes 24.

Coffee-Walnut Cookies

8 ounces plain flour, sifted
8 ounces butter, softened
5 ounces icing sugar, sifted
1 egg yolk
Few drops vanilla extract

5 ounces coarsely chopped
  walnuts
2 tablespoons medium-ground
  fresh coffee
4 ounces walnut pieces

1 Preheat oven to 350F (180C). Butter several baking sheets.

2 Into a bowl, sift flour. Add butter, icing sugar, egg yolk and vanilla. Mix well, then mix in the chopped walnuts and coffee with your hands.

3 Place heaped teaspoonfuls of mixture on prepared baking sheets. Flatten slightly and top each mound with a walnut piece. Bake for 12 to 15 minutes, until just starting to colour. Cool on baking sheets for a few minutes, then transfer to wire racks to cool completely.

Makes 28 to 30.

Lemon Shortbread

4 ounces butter, softened
2 ounces caster sugar
5 ounces plain flour
1/4 teaspoon ground nutmeg

2 tablespoons cornflour
Grated zest of 1 lemon
TO FINISH: Caster sugar and
   grated nutmeg, for
   sprinkling

1 In a bowl, beat butter with sugar until creamy. Into another bowl, sift flour and
nutmeg, then add cornflour and lemon zest. Blend in creamed butter and sugar with
a spoon, then work with your hands to form a soft dough.

2 In a lightly floured surface, knead until smooth. Roll out to a smooth circle, about 6
inches in diameter. Very lightly flour a 7-inch shortbread mould. Place shortbread,
smooth side down, in mould. Press out to fit the mould exactly. Very carefully remove
shortbread onto a baking sheet. Refrigerate for 1 hour. (If you do not have a shortbread
mould, shape dough into a neat circle. Place on baking sheet, prick well with a fork,
then pinch edge to decorate.)

3 Preheat oven to 325F (160C). Bake shortbread for 35 to 40 minutes, until cooked
through but still pale in colour. As soon as shortbread is removed from oven, sprinkle
lightly with sugar and nutmeg. Cool on baking sheet about 20 minutes, then very
carefully transfer to a wire rack to cool completely.

Makes 1.

Chocolate Chequerboards

6 ounces butter, softened	1 pound 2 ounces plain flour
6 ounces caster sugar	2 teaspoons baking powder
Few drops vanilla essence	1 teaspoon milk
2 eggs	2 tablespoons cocoa powder

1 Grease several baking sheets. Divide butter and sugar equally between 2 bowls.

2 To make vanilla dough, in a bowl, beat half of the butter and sugar until light and fluffy. Beat in vanilla and 1 egg. In another bowl, sift half of the flour and 1 teaspoon of baking powder. Blend in with a spoon, then work by hand to form a smooth dough. Make chocolate dough in same way with remaining butter, sugar and egg, adding milk and sifting in cocoa powder with remaining flour and baking powder. Divide each portion of dough into 4 equal pieces.

3 In a floured surface, roll each piece of dough into a rope 12 inches long. Place 1 chocolate rope next to a vanilla one. Place a chocolate one on top of the vanilla one and a vanilla one on top of the chocolate. Press firmly together to form a square. Wrap in cling film. Repeat with remaining dough. Refrigerate 1 hour. Preheat oven to 350F (180C). Cut dough into 48 slices and place on baking sheets. Bake 20 minutes until lightly browned. Cool on wire racks.

Makes 48.

Double Chocolate Cookies

4 ounces butter
2 ounces granulated sugar
2 ounces soft brown sugar
1 egg, beaten
Few drops vanilla essence

$4^1/_2$ ounces plain flour
2 tablespoons cocoa powder
$^1/_2$ teaspoon baking soda
5 ounces white chocolate
    chips

1 Preheat oven to 350F (180C). Butter several baking sheets.

2 In a bowl, beat butter with sugars until creamy. Gradually beat in egg and vanilla
essence. Into another bowl, sift flour, cocoa powder and baking soda. Mix well, then
stir in chocolate chips.

3 Drop teaspoonfuls of dough, well spaced out, onto prepared baking sheets. Bake for
10 to 12 minutes, until firm. Cool on baking sheets a few minutes, then remove to
wire racks to cool completely.

Makes about 48.

Lemon Curd

4 lemons
12 ounces caster sugar

4 ounces butter
4 eggs, beaten

1 Into a heatproof bowl, finely grate zest of lemons. Squeeze lemons and pour juice into bowl. Stir in sugar. Cut butter into small pieces and add to other ingredients.

2 Set bowl over a saucepan one-quarter filled with simmering water and stir until butter has melted and sugar dissolved. Strain eggs into lemon mixture.

3 Cook gently, stirring frequently, for 10 to 15 minutes, until mixture is thick and creamy. Pour into warm jars and seal while hot. Refrigerate.

Makes about 1 1/2 pounds.

Variations: For Lime Curd, use limes instead of lemons. For Lemon & Elderflower Curd, add 2 handfuls of elderberry flowers, well shaken and flowers removed from stems, after adding butter.

Apple Butter

40 fluid ounces dry cider
2¹/₂ pounds dessert apples
1 pound cooking apples
Granulated sugar
Grated zest and juice of ¹/₂
    orange

Grated zest and juice of
    ¹/₂ lemon
¹/₂ teaspoon ground cinnamon
¹/₂ teaspoon ground cloves

1 Into a large saucepan, put cider. Boil rapidly until reduced by one-third. With a knife, peel, core and slice apples, then add to pan.

2 If necessary, add enough water to just cover apples. Half cover pan and simmer until apples are very soft and pulpy and well reduced. Stir occasionally and crush pulp down in pan as it cooks. Measure pulp and process to a puree if it is lumpy. Return to saucepan. Add 10 ounces of sugar for every 20 fluid ounces of apple pulp. Stir in orange and lemon zests and juices, cinnamon and cloves.

3 Cook gently until sugar has dissolved. Simmer, stirring frequently, until most moisture has been driven off. The mixture is ready when a spoon drawn across the surface leaves an impression. Spoon into clean, warm jars and store in the refrigerator. Once a jar is opened, apple butter should be consumed within 3 to 4 days.

Makes 4 or 5 small jars.

Cumberland Rum Butter

4 ounces butter, softened
8 ounces dark brown sugar
1/4 teaspoon ground cinnamon
2 tablespoons dark rum

TO SERVE: Hot toast, muffins
  or crumpets
TO DECORATE: orange zest

1 Into a bowl, put butter and beat until soft. Gradually beat in sugar.

2 Gradually beat in the cinnamon and rum. Pile mixture into a small dish. Cover and refrigerate until firm. Decorate with orange zest. Serve with hot toast, muffins or crumpets.

Makes 6 to 8 servings.

Variation: For Anchovy Butter, instead of sugar, cinnamon and rum, work 11/2 ounces drained, tinned anchovies into butter. Serve on toast.

Iced Rose Tea

1¹/₂ ounces Ceylon breakfast
    tea
35 fluid ounces lukewarm
    water
Sugar, to taste

Few drops rosewater, to taste
12 ice cubes
6 mint sprigs
Fresh rose petals

1 Into a bowl, put tea. Pour warm
water over tea and let stand
overnight.

2 Strain tea into a large pitcher. Stir in
sugar and rosewater, then add ice
cubes. Place a mint sprig and a few rose
petals in each of 6 glasses. Pour tea on
top.

Makes 6 servings.

Variations: For Vanilla Iced Tea, omit
rosewater. Instead, put a vanilla pod in
the bowl with tea to soak overnight.
Remove it before serving. For Mint Tea,
omit the rosewater and rose petals. Put a
mint sprig in bowl with tea to soak
overnight. Remove it before serving.
Place a fresh mint sprig in each glass.

Spiced Tea

Small piece root ginger, peeled
4 whole cloves
1-inch stick cinnamon
2 tablespoons Ceylon tea
2 ounces caster sugar

2¹/₂ fluid ounces orange juice
Juice of ¹/₂ lemon
TO DECORATE: 4 to 6
    cinnamon sticks

1 Bruise ginger. In a saucepan, combine ginger, cloves, cinnamon and 4¹/₂ cups of cold water. Bring to the boil.

2 Into a heatproof bowl, put tea. Pour boiling spiced water over tea, then steep for 5 minutes. Add sugar and stir until dissolved, then stir in orange and lemon juices.

3 Preheat before serving, but do not simmer or boil. Strain spiced tea into heatproof glasses. Serve with a cinnamon stick in each glass.

Makes 4 to 6 servings.

Note: This drink is also delicious served chilled.

Variation: To make Party Punch, add extra sugar, to taste, then just before serving, add 10 fluid ounces of rum.

Serves 4 to 6.

Tennis Cup

8 ounces granulated sugar
1 lemon
2 oranges
2 bottles of red or white wine
20 fluid ounces soda water

TO DECORATE: Thin cucumber
  and orange slices
Borage flowers or violets,
  if available

1 Into a saucepan, put sugar and water. Cook over low heat, stirring, until sugar has dissolved. Bring to a boil, then boil until syrup reaches 220F (105C).

2 With a potato peeler, thinly pare rind from lemon and oranges. Add to syrup and simmer gently for 10 minutes. Set aside until completely cold.

3 Squeeze juice from lemon and oranges and strain into syrup, then pour in the wine and refrigerate until chilled. Just before serving, add soda water. Pour into glasses. Decorate with cucumber and orange slices and borage sprigs or violets.

Makes about 70 fluid ounces.

Summer Tea Cup

1 Lapsang Souchong tea bag
20 fluid ounces boiling water
4 teaspoons brown sugar
10 fluid ounces pineapple juice
2¹/₂ fluid ounces white rum

20 fluid ounces ginger ale
Ice cubes
TO DECORATE: Pieces of fresh
pineapple

1 In a heatproof bowl, place tea bag and boiling water.

2 Leave tea to steep for 5 minutes, then remove tea bag. Stir in brown sugar and leave until cold. Stir in pineapple juice and rum into tea.

3 Just before serving, pour ginger ale into tea. Add ice cubes. Place a few pieces of pineapple in each glass and pour in the chilled tea.

Makes about 52 fluid ounces.

Old-Fashioned Lemonade

3 lemons
4 ounces sugar

TO FINISH: Ice
Mint sprigs
Lemon slices

1 Using a potato peeler, thinly pare rind from lemons and put in a heatproof bowl or large pitcher with sugar. Squeeze juice from lemons into a bowl and set aside.

2 Bring 30 fluid ounces of water to the boil and pour over lemon peel and sugar. Stir to dissolve sugar, then let cool completely. Add lemon juice and strain into a pitcher. Refrigerate until chilled. Serve in ice-filled tumblers, decorate with mint and lemon slices.

Makes 6 servings.

Variations: To make Pink Lemonade, add just enough pink grenadine syrup to each glass to give lemonade a pale pink colour. Omit mint and lemon slices and decorate each glass with a cherry. To make Orangeade, use 3 oranges and 1 lemon instead of 3 lemons. Omit mint and lemon slices and decorate with orange slices.

Grapefruit Barley Water

2 ounces pearl
    barley
2 ounces sugar

2 pink grapefruit
TO DECORATE: Mint
    leaves

1 Into a saucepan, put barley. Just cover with cold water and bring to the boil. Pour barley into a strainer and rinse under cold water.

2 Return barley to saucepan. Add 2 1/2 cups cold water and bring to boil again. Cover and simmer for 1 hour. Strain liquid into a pitcher, stir in the sugar and leave until completely cold.

3 Squeeze juice from grapefruit and add to cooled barley water. Refrigerate until chilled. Serve decorated with mint leaves.

Makes about 20 fluid ounces.

Variation: To make Lemon Barley Water, use 2 lemons instead of grapefruit.

Index